Open to Me the Gates

Gradye Parsons

Published by Witherspoon Press, a ministry of the General Assembly Mission Council, Presbyterian Church (U.S.A.), 100 Witherspoon St., Louisville, Kentucky.

PRINTED IN THE UNITED STATES OF AMERICA

gamc.pcusa.org/ministries/curriculum/witherspoon-press/

Introduction

Many years ago, I visited a couple who had traveled from California to Tennessee in the early days of the automobile. They talked about the poor condition of the roads and the lack of clear directions.

One thing they said really stuck with me: "Sometimes, the road we were on stopped at the entrance to a farmer's pasture. We would have to open the gate to the field to continue our trip. At times, we couldn't see that the road went across the pasture; we just had to take the folks' word for it."

The journey through Lent often involves a series of paths that require us to pass through a gate so that we can continue moving forward in faith. Sometimes we face the challenge of whether we have the willpower to go ahead or detour to an easier road when it comes to any Lenten disciplines we have begun. And sometimes God closes the journey ahead and sends us in a different direction altogether.

I have chosen six biblical stories that involve gates. In the context of those stories and with a little imagination, these gates may help us reflect on who we are and the nature of our faith.

In 1 Kings, we see how city gates can be a great equalizer.

In Joshua, we explore what happens when a gate is closed, leaving no apparent escape route for those who are trapped.

In Amos, we observe how gates help to make visible those whom society has made invisible.

In Acts, two disciples point out the threshold of the beautiful gate that we all need to cross to be faithful.

On Palm Sunday, we see the gate of commitment, ready as we are—or not.

Finally, we celebrate the Good Shepherd, who is Way and Truth and Life—as well as Gate for the Christian community.

Over the course of these stories, you will be asked to consider what gate stands between you and the person God is calling you to be. What will it take for you to cross the threshold?

Chapter 1

Meeting at the Gates

Then the word of the Lord came to him, saying, "Go now to Zarephath, which belongs to Sidon, and live there; for I have commanded a widow there to feed you." So he set out and went to Zarephath. When he came to the gate of the town, a widow was there gathering sticks; he called to her and said, "Bring me a little water in a vessel, so that I may drink." As she was going to bring it, he called to her and said, "Bring me a morsel of bread in your hand." But she said, "As the Lord your God lives, I have nothing baked, only a handful of meal in a jar, and a little oil in a jug; I am now gathering a couple of sticks, so that I may go home and prepare it for myself and my son, that we may eat it, and die." Elijah said to her, "Do not be afraid; go and do as you have said; but first make me a little cake of it and bring it to me, and afterwards make something for yourself and your son. For thus says the Lord the God of Israel: The jar of meal will not be emptied and the jug of oil will not fail until the day that the Lord sends rain on the earth." She went and did as Elijah said, so that she as well as he and her household ate for many days. The jar of meal was not emptied, neither did the jug of oil fail, according to the word of the Lord that he spoke by Elijah.

—1 Kings 17:8–16

Gates: The Great Equalizers

No matter who we are, or our stations in life, gates are great equalizers.

The rich ride through the gates, as do the poor.
The healthy ride through the gates, as well as the sick.
Couples with new babies ride through the gates and so do mourners in funeral processions.
People with power ride through the gates, as do the marginalized.
Brides ride through the gates, and so do widows.
Some walk through the gates in silk slippers; others pass through on bare feet.

Gates form part of the boundary of a town, mainly determining who is in and who is out. Everyone enters and leaves village life through them. They mark territory, provide protection, and shut out trouble. They are gathering spots; and in their shade, they once served as the courtroom, where people sought justice.

Gates are equalizers.

So many things divide us. Surveys will analyze how brown-eyed, left-handed people who were born in the fifties are different from green-eyed, right-handed people who were born in the sixties. If you identify with a particular political stereotype, then you must like this; if you don't, you must like that. Such information may be useful for some. However, it tends to create a sense that we are all so different from one another, there is no way we can have the same needs and wants.

> **The gate was an opening in the ancient city wall through which almost all citizens passed daily to get to their fields or to take care of business inside the city.**

But we do.
We all need to be loved.
We all need to feel safe.
We all need to be healthy.
We all need to pay our bills.

We all need to know that our families are safe.
We all need to feel appreciated.
We all need to be forgiven.
We all suffer heartache.
We all mourn.
We all experience hunger.
We all suffer fear.
We all fear being alone.

No matter who we are, or our stations in life, gates are great equalizers.

Elijah and the Widow

The story of Elijah and King Ahab reads like a soap opera. Moments of public courage meet moments of private desperation.

King Ahab comes by his role as villain in the oldest of traditions—he inherited it from his father, King Omri. His father had overthrown King Zimri, who had overthrown King Asa. Omri had made Samaria the capital of Israel.

"Omri did what was evil in the sight of the Lord; he did more evil than all who went before him" (1 Kings 16:25). How would you like to read that statement on your parent's tombstone? Along comes Ahab; like all sons before and since, he seeks to outdo his father. He achieves that goal! "Ahab son of Omri did evil in the sight of the Lord more than all who were before him" (1 Kings 16:30).

Ahab adds to his reputation by marrying Jezebel, daughter of the king of the Sidonians. She brings with her to Samaria her religion of worshiping Baal, the god of rain, thunder, fertility, and agriculture. This provokes Yahweh, the God of Israel, to great anger, so God sends the prophet Elijah.

Elijah confronts Ahab and this new religion. Elijah declares that a drought with neither dew nor rain will happen until Elijah commands it to stop. Ahab is furious, which prompts Elijah to hide in a ravine where there is a small stream. Ravens bring him bread and meat, and the stream provides water—until it dries up.

Then the Lord tells Elijah to go to Zarephath, where a widow will feed and take care of him. Undoubtedly, at that point, Elijah must have said, "What? How is that again?" Elijah knows that Zarephath is in Sidon, which happens to be the home country of Jezebel. The widow is probably dependent on charity herself. How could she help Elijah?

Help from a Surprising Source

You've probably had the experience of being mad at a colleague. You leave the office and decide to take your family out for dinner to get your mind off your anger. You settle down at your table, looking forward to a nice meal. When you look up, your colleague and his family sit at the table next to yours.

You pick up the phone without checking caller ID and end up in a long conversation with your long-lost, lonely cousin.

You stand before the drink machine and realize you don't have exact change. The woman whose raise you just turned down offers to help you.

You've decided to make morning devotions your Lenten discipline. The first morning is the day the batteries in the alarm clock go dead.

God must have a whole room of agents whose sole purpose is to work little moments into our lives in which the better half of our selves has to deal with our worse half.

Elijah goes to drought-stricken Zarephath. There, at the gate, he immediately sees the widow, who is picking up sticks for her cooking fire. He can see plainly that she is poor and desperate.

> **In times of peace, the gate was the center of city life.**

The prophet asks her for water. She agrees, but on her way, he stops her and asks for more. "And while you're at it, bake me some bread."

Then Elijah gets the rest of the story. This widow—the one who is going to rescue him—is down to her last measures of meal and oil. She plans to make bread for herself and her son, after which they will silently wait for starvation to take them.

Zarephath is a small town about a mile from the Mediterranean coast. Its name means "a workshop for refining or smelting metals." Surely, others in the town had more means than the widow had and were better prepared to help Elijah. After all, the widow was down to her last pan of cornbread.

Elijah realizes he cannot trust his eyes, so he must trust God. God brings together two improbable people—the widow and the prophet. The widow hides Elijah in her home; Elijah gives the widow the means to survive the drought.

Jesus and the Widow

Soon afterwards Jesus went to a town called Nain, and his disciples and a large crowd went with him. As he approached the gate of the town, a man who had died was being carried out. He was his mother's only son, and she was a widow; and with her was a large crowd from the town. When the Lord saw her, he had compassion for her and said to her, "Do not weep." Then he came forward and touched the bier, and the bearers stood still. And he said, "Young man, I say to you, rise!" The dead man sat up and began to speak, and Jesus gave him to his mother. Fear seized all of them; and they glorified God, saying, "A great prophet has risen among us!" and "God has looked favorably on his people!" This word about him spread throughout Judea and all the surrounding country.

—Luke 7:11–17

Luke 7 presents another simple story of a meeting at the gate. Jesus and the disciples approach the town of Nain. Imagine the scene. Thirteen men enter the town. James and John, the "sons of thunder," elbow each other to get further ahead in line, while Matthew works to avoid looks from his former fellow tax collector. Judas jingles the money box.

Approaching them is a funeral procession. A widow has lost her only son, which could mean she will lose all of her future security—perhaps even her home. Jesus has compassion for her and stops his band of disciples. He reaches out to touch the funeral bier and gives the command "Young man, I say to you, rise!" (Luke 7:14). The young man rises and is returned to his mother. The town spreads the word about Jesus throughout the surrounding country.

The dead were buried beyond the gates.

Open to Me the Gates

Gates of Opportunity

These two stories contain powerful avenues for our Lenten journey:

Suffering widows
Starving children
Mourning mothers
A prophet
Jesus
Miracles
Compassion
Raising from the dead

However, I am struck by the role of the city gate in both stories.

The widows at the gate are in the midst of suffering. One is near starvation; the other near homelessness. The first widow meets a prophet on the run; the second meets a Savior on the way to the cross. God uses their willingness to approach the prophet and the Savior to redirect their paths toward a brighter future.

When you are down to your last jar of meal and oil, it is hard to care for anyone else. When you feel like a desert inside, it is hard to offer the stranger a drink of cool water. When we are so wrapped up in our own Lenten discipline that we do not see the other, it is a struggle to hear the pain of the other.

That is one reason God gives us the church. Although the church cannot mend every wound, patch every tear, pay everyone's bills, or prevent every heartbreak, the church is the place where we can stand with one another. It is the place where being together gives us a sense of the gates—yes, I am human, broken, and empty, but I am not alone. The church is there with me to heal and to offer forgiveness.

I rarely see a meaningful moment on a television medical drama. However, I will have to confess that the writers for *Grey's Anatomy* captured just such a moment.

An airplane had crashed into the harbor. The hospital was to be the trauma center where all of the survivors would be brought and families could gather for information. Then comes the sobering news: no survivors. The doctors who had prepared to do lifesaving surgeries become grief counselors instead. One by one, the families are notified and most leave the hospital.

Suddenly, word comes that a survivor has been found—a young girl traveling home from visiting her grandparents. However, none of her family has arrived yet. As the husband of a couple that had lingered stands to leave, his wife won't budge.

"What if that had been our son?" she asks. "Would we want him to be here all alone?" She and the others sit and wait.

Eventually the young girl's mother arrives. The woman who refused to leave offers comfort to the mother while relaying nothing of her own grief. In fact, no one tells the mother that her child is the only survivor.

The remaining families had nothing inside. They had all gone through an experience of loss and suffering. Yet they found they could still offer the ministry of presence.

Stand by Me

Charles Albert Tindley was born the son of slaves. After the American Civil War, he and his wife moved to Philadelphia, where he worked as a janitor in a church. He taught himself to read and write. He wanted to be a minister, so he took correspondence courses until he was able to pass the required examinations. He eventually returned as a minister to the church where he had been a janitor.

Under his ministry the church grew to over 10,000 members.

Tindley was the author of many gospel hymns, including what became "We Shall Overcome." One of his famous hymns calls upon God to stand by us during the trials of life. Many times, God sends us to stand by one another during those trials. I invite you to read this great old hymn in that way, thinking about the people who have stood by you when you needed them.

Stand by Me

When the storms of life are raging, stand by me;
When the storms of life are raging, stand by me.
When the world is tossing me
    like a ship upon the sea,
Thou who rulest wind and water, stand by me.

In the midst of tribulation, stand by me;
In the midst of tribulation, stand by me.
When the hosts of hell assail,
    and my strength begins to fail,
Thou who never lost a battle, stand by me.

In the midst of faults and failures, stand by me;
In the midst of faults and failures, stand by me.
When I do the best I can,
    and my friends misunderstand,
Thou who knowest all about me, stand by me.

In the midst of persecution, stand by me;
In the midst of persecution, stand by me.
When my foes in battle array
    undertake to stop my way,
Thou who saved Paul and Silas,[1] stand by me.

When I'm growing old and feeble, stand by me;
When I'm growing old and feeble, stand by me.
When my life becomes a burden,
    and I'm nearing chilly Jordan,
O Thou "Lily of the Valley,"[2] stand by me.[3]

Chapter 2

The Surprising Gate

Then Joshua son of Nun sent two men secretly from Shittim as spies, saying, "Go, view the land, especially Jericho." So they went, and entered the house of a prostitute whose name was Rahab, and spent the night there. The king of Jericho was told, "Some Israelites have come here tonight to search out the land." Then the king of Jericho sent orders to Rahab, "Bring out the men who have come to you, who entered your house, for they have come only to search out the whole land." But the woman took the two men and hid them. Then she said, "True, the men came to me, but I did not know where they came from. And when it was time to close the gate at dark, the men went out. Where the men went I do not know. Pursue them quickly, for you can overtake them." She had, however, brought them up to the roof and hidden them with the stalks of flax that she had laid out on the roof. So the men pursued them on the way to the Jordan as far as the fords. As soon as the pursuers had gone out, the gate was shut.

Before they went to sleep, she came up to them on the roof and said to the men: "I know that the Lord has given you the land, and that dread of you has fallen on us, and that all the inhabitants of the land melt in fear before you. For we have heard how the Lord dried up the water of the Red Sea before you when you came out of Egypt, and what you did to the two kings of the Amorites that were beyond the Jordan, to Sihon and Og, whom you utterly destroyed. As soon as we heard it, our hearts melted, and there was no courage left in any of us because of you. The Lord your God is indeed God in heaven above and on earth below. Now then, since I have dealt kindly with you, swear to me by the Lord that you in turn will deal kindly with my family. Give me a sign of good faith that you will spare my father and mother, my brothers and sisters, and all who belong to them, and deliver our lives from death." The men said to her, "Our life for yours! If you do not tell this business of ours, then we will deal kindly and faithfully with you when the Lord gives us the land." Then she let them down by a rope through the window, for her house was on the outer side of the city wall and she resided within the wall itself.

—Joshua 2:1–15

Retracing Joshua's Steps

Readers of the first chapter of Joshua have to know that something big is coming. Moses has just died, Joshua is the new leader of the Israelites, and the Promised Land is literally in sight after forty long years of wandering through the wilderness.

"Be strong and courageous."

Not one, but four times Joshua shares these words with those he has assembled (Joshua 1:6, 7, 9, 18). I imagine it was an admonition that Joshua recalled as he prepared to send two spies into the land across the Jordan River to scout out the inhabitants. He himself had been in their shoes in an earlier time. He was among a group of men that Moses had sent into Canaan with a similar charge (Numbers 13:17–20). Joshua

Joshua and the earlier group of spies had done as they were told. Their report back to Moses contained great news. They had found a fertile land: a single cluster of grapes they had cut down required two men to carry it on a pole between them.

Then the spies talked about the inhabitants of Canaan. "We are not able to go up against this people, for they are stronger than we" (Numbers 13:31). They went on to describe the inhabitants as those who seemed like giants, while they seemed like grasshoppers.

The ever-murmuring crowd cried out when they heard the report, fearing they would soon be back in slavery. So plans for the invasion were halted.

Joshua could not believe what he was hearing. He and fellow spy Caleb tore their clothes and shouted, "You chicken-hearted people!" (paraphrased), to which the crowd responded with threats to stone them.

So if Joshua needed to be reminded to be brave before he sent in spies this time, it was warranted. He carefully picked two men and sent them toward the land across the Jordan.

Infiltrating Jericho

The two young men selected by Joshua had been born in the desert during the wandering years. They had lived their entire lives in a large tent city that was divided into twelve tribes. No one who had escaped from Egypt was still alive, except for Joshua and Caleb.

These young men had been raised on a steady diet of manna and quail. (After so many years, I envision some kind of competition among the Israelites to see who had the most unusual quail recipe.) Everyone knew everyone else in the tent city. As with all nomadic tribes, the rituals of daily life had few diversions, so that every move and every new tent city they pitched was a routine matter.

When the two spies crossed the Jordan, they found a very different world. They saw farmers tending fields and shepherds tending sheep. They saw villages where carpenters constructed ox bows and wheels for their carts. They saw houses with roofs and gardens.

Then they crested a hill and saw Jericho.

I imagine these two young men coming to a halt when they see the walled city of Jericho. I grew up in a small town in the middle of Tennessee where the tallest structure was the silo at the chicken feed plant. Every so often, like most parents from small towns in that part of Tennessee, my parents would pile my brother and me into the family station wagon and drive the two-lane state highways to Nashville. One of the highlights of the trip was to be the first to spot and exclaim, "I see the L&C" (the Life and Casualty Insurance building), which was the tallest structure in Nashville for years.

Many entrances to city gates were built with steps or a right-angle turn to make them easier to defend.

Haven with a Harlot

As the two men approached Jericho, their senses had to have been on overload as they took in the sights, smells, and sounds of the city while sizing up its defenses. Being two young men from the desert, it is not a complete surprise that they got no further than their first true distraction—Rahab the harlot. The text records nothing of their examination of the rest of Jericho. We are left with the impression that this was it.

We need not try to redefine Rahab—although some doubt that a person with such an occupation would have lived in tightly controlled Jericho. History has not found a need to rename her Rahab the hairdresser or Rahab the real estate agent. She is Rahab the harlot, plain and simple. Well, maybe not so simple. She apparently owned her home, had time to make cloth out of flax, and communicated equally with young nomads and kings.

In God's great irony, these two young sons of the Ten Commandments suddenly found themselves dependent on the trustworthiness of someone who had probably broken most of what was written on those holy stone tablets. While the two young rubes from the desert were spying on Jericho, Jericho had been spying on them. Word reached the king of the city, who might have had his own spies across the Jordan spying on Joshua and the tent city, for all we know.

The king sent word to Rahab: "Bring out the men who have come to you, who entered your house, for they have come only to search out the whole land" (Joshua 2:3).

Rahab, who was used to lying for the king, apparently had no trouble lying to him. She claimed that the men had left, but there was still time to catch them. In the meantime, she hid the frightened young men under the stalks of flax she had drying on the roof. The king's men believed her story and headed toward the Jordan as far as the fords. "As soon as the pursuers had gone out, the gate was shut" (Joshua 2:7).

The gate was shut.

When closed, the doors were barred from the inside with a heavy beam or metal bar inserted in slots. They could not be pushed in from the outside because they rested against an inner doorstop.

What Do You Do When the Gate Is Shut?

My wife and I raised our children with many basic instructions, wise sayings, and other general parenting pearls. One of those pearls was: when you are making plans, always, always have a plan B because sometimes plan A will not work. There may even be moments in life when you have to go all the way to plan Z.

Where in the world is forward and how do we move in that direction when the gate is shut on plans A through Z? We can't go back, or even sideways, and we realize that the capacity is not in us to see the next step.

What do you do when the gate is shut? The young nomads made themselves vulnerable—which I am guessing may have been as difficult for them as it is for us.

The space between verses 7 and 8 is as blank and empty as the future seemed to be for these two young nomads. They had obviously failed as spies. They were in a very strange city—on top of their first roof. They were probably trying hard not to move under the flax as their hearts pounded. They had no reason not to expect a spear to pierce their backs at any moment. Moreover, they were dependent on a Jericho harlot for their very lives.

Being vulnerable is, by far, not our favorite thing to do. Being vulnerable means we might get hurt. It means someone might see how scared we are. It means showing our weak side. Being vulnerable means having open hands and wide-open eyes (or, perhaps, shut at times) and allowing what is to come, to come.

The Gate That Is Revealed

Fearful, the two young spies were forced to be still underneath the pile of flax on Rahab's roof. At times, we may need to force ourselves to be still, as well, though for different reasons.

We live in a world full of noise. For many of us, our internal lives are just as noisy, which can become a steady hum of distraction—those constant whispers of: Have you done this? Can you do that? Am I loved? Am I worthy enough to join the chorus?

To be still and to listen to, and for, God is no easy trick. Sometimes it seems as though God resorts to shutting all of the gates so that we will be still and shut down the noise. Then the Holy Spirit can finally get in a word and a gate opens.

The spies did not know where, how, or if they would escape their predicament. While none of us has been in that particular situation, we have had those moments! And, like the spies, we find that sometimes the gate that opens is a surprise.

The two spies had two gates that opened for them. The first was Rahab; the second, a rope.

Rahab's life and experiences were different from those of the young men in every way imaginable. Yet she was pivotal in guiding the two to safety. We have the impulse to think—perhaps assume—that God

Open to Me the Gates

will speak to us, care for us, and guide us through other Christians who are like us. Sometimes, usually surprisingly, we gain insights from and are touched by people we could never imagine doing so.

The rope itself needs no explanation in the story. Yet it was the mechanism for these two tent dwellers to do something they had never done before, which was to climb out of a second-story window. What might God be asking you to do that you have never done before? What might your "rope" be?

If You But Trust

Georg Neumark wrote hymns in the seventeenth century during the Thirty Years' War. When he was eighteen years old, he was traveling to a city to study when he was robbed of all of his possessions. He spent the next two years looking for work. Not long after he secured a tutoring job, he wrote this hymn based on Psalm 55:22.

If You But Trust
If thou but trust in God to guide thee,
With hopeful heart through all thy ways,
God will give strength, whate'er betide thee,
To bear thee through the evil days.
Who trusts in God's unchanging love
Builds on the rock that nought can move.

Only be still, and wait God's leisure
In cheerful hope, with heart content
To take whate'er thy Keeper's pleasure
And all discerning love hath sent.
No doubt our inmost wants are clear
To One who holds us always dear.

Sing, pray, and swerve not from God's ways,
Bur do thine own part faithfully;
Trust the rich promises of grace,
So shall they be fulfilled in thee.
God never yet forsook at need
The soul secured by trust indeed.[4]

Chapter 3

Justice at the Gates

For thus says the Lord to the house of Israel: Seek me and live; but do not seek Bethel, and do not enter into Gilgal or cross over to Beer-sheba; for Gilgal shall surely go into exile, and Bethel shall come to nothing.

Seek the Lord and live, or he will break out against the house of Joseph like fire, and it will devour Bethel, with no one to quench it. Ah, you that turn justice to wormwood, and bring righteousness to the ground!

The one who made the Pleiades and Orion, and turns deep darkness into the morning, and darkens the day into night, who calls for the waters of the sea, and pours them out on the surface of the earth, the Lord is his name, who makes destruction flash out against the strong, so that destruction comes upon the fortress.

They hate the one who reproves in the gate, and they abhor the one who speaks the truth. Therefore because you trample on the poor and take from them levies of grain, you have built houses of hewn stone, but you shall not live in them; you have planted pleasant vineyards, but you shall not drink their wine. For I know how many are your transgressions, and how great are your sins—you who afflict the righteous, who take a bribe, and push aside the needy in the gate. Therefore the prudent will keep silent in such a time; for it is an evil time.

Seek good and not evil, that you may live; and so the Lord, the God of hosts, will be with you, just as you have said. Hate evil and love good, and establish justice in the gate; it may be that the Lord, the God of hosts, will be gracious to the remnant of Joseph.

—Amos 5:4–15

Gates of Injustice

Lent tends to begin well. We start our disciplines and the first days are fine. Others we know who have made similar commitments appear to be OK with their new do-withouts or their will-do-betters.

Then it happens. The pull back to the familiar begins to creep in slowly. We drop one new good habit and pick up an old one. Eventually, we end up back where we started. The only aspect of Lent that has any regular focus for us is Sunday, leaving Monday through Saturday seemingly untouched by the season.

Lent is a hard teacher. It reveals our will and level of willingness, or lack thereof, to work to live out one of the forty-day journeys in the Bible. We begin with great intentions and, more times than not, end up disappointing ourselves.

In the story from Amos, we see what can happen with similar good intentions in a community built around God—how a society can become blind to its own citizens and its own unrighteousness.

The gates of injustice reveal all.

Amos's World

The Northern Kingdom of Israel experienced a bit of a boom back when Jeroboam was king. It was a time of peace and prosperity. Trade and agriculture grew, as did Israel's borders.

People made fortunes. Well, some people did. Many did not. What had been the traditional culture of Israel, where most families were living at about the same level, disappeared slowly.

Towns began to change, too. Archaeologists who have uncovered communities that predate the era of Jeroboam have found that most homes were about the same size. In ruins from Jeroboam's time,

Elders administered justice in the gate.

some sections of towns had large homes; others had nothing more than shacks.

This shift of some having more and many having less in society extended beyond the town walls into the surrounding countryside. Absentee property owners now owned plots of land that had been handed down through the generations. Farmers no longer worked their own farms. The fragility of subsistence farming was used by others to snatch away land and to put people into indentured slavery.

This was the world of Amos the prophet.

One staple of life—the gates into towns and cities—remained unchanged. There were often four rather elaborate gates with chambers. In some cities, the chambers were large side rooms where the town-square life of the community was conducted. Gathered around were tax collectors, gossipers, beggars, and, if one was blessed, justice.

One or more of the chambers were used as courtrooms. The town elders heard the complaints and rendered judgments. This is the backdrop for the problem described in the text from Amos:

Ah, you that turn justice to wormwood, and bring righteousness to the ground!

They hate the one who reproves in the gate, and they abhor the one who speaks the truth.

Hate evil and love good, and establish justice in the gate . . . .

—Amos 5:7, 10, 15

Justice and righteousness are not two words for the same thing. Rather, they work together like two ingredients in a pie. The person who has been wronged seeks justice, seeking to have restored whatever has been taken—for instance, possessions, rights, or health. The person who has committed the wrongdoing needs to be restored to righteousness by righting both the wrong and, more importantly, the relationship.

It Matters to God

The relationship of God's people to one another matters to God, and what was happening in Israel was obviously not sitting well with their Creator. Amos uses very serious language to describe God's displeasure:

Seek the Lord and live, or [God] will break out against the house of Joseph like fire . . . . (5:6);

For I know how many are your transgressions, and how great are your sins—you who afflict the righteous, who take a bribe, and push aside the needy in the gate (5:12).

Can you imagine the scenes?

- A lender gives money to a poor farmer to buy seed for his field, then demands that the money be repaid before the crop is harvested.
- A widow sells woven goods from a little stall that is in the way of a new house someone wants to build.
- Parents borrow a little money to buy sandals for their children, only to watch their children be sold into slavery because they borrowed a little money.

These changes in society did not happen all at once, but over time—a little here and some there. One person was denied justice. No one cried foul. Another refused to live a righteous life and was still seated among the town leaders. Nobody raised the issue. Yet slowly the web of relationships was realigned. Certain people talked only to certain people, which meant that other people did not speak to them.

The Least among You

Another abomination during Jeroboam's reign was a foundering religious life. The religion center in Israel was at Bethel. Festivals were well attended and ever more glorious. And why not? God was giving Israel this era of great prosperity. So, people donned all of the bling that came their way from God's abundance and went to Bethel to show off how good God had been to them.

Kings sat at the gate to meet their subjects or administer justice.

The story of religious people acting in an unrighteous manner is not limited to ancient Israel.

A while back, my wife, son, and I went out to eat after church. It was a pretty day and worship had been especially good. Our young server, complete with tattoos and piercings, gave us menus along with her spiel about the day's specials. I made some lame joke that we had just come from church and we knew we should be good tippers. She turned slowly. "Well," she said, appearing sadly resigned, "that would be different. Most church folks tell me they can't leave a tip because they left all of their loose change at church."

These would be church folks who had just finished passing the peace of Christ and singing praises to God. These same folks would turn right around and dismiss this young woman. Why? It is because she was invisible to them.

She was invisible to them in the same way that the poor, the widow, and the orphan were invisible to the judges at the gates back in ancient Israel. People become invisible when they are no longer viewed as equals and worthy of relationship. They become invisible when our sense of righteousness does not compute into right living with them. We cannot see the Christ in them if we cannot really see them at all.

> **Prophets spoke against the perversion of justice "in the gate."**

The Gift of Gates

One of the gifts of gates is that they make visible what or who is invisible. The poor supplicant who is pushed to live in squalor is now seen. The little farmer with his calluses is now seen. The widow who became invisible when her husband died is now seen.

Those who live unrighteously are now seen, as well. The person who built the grand new house where three simple homes once stood is seen. The owner of the new stylish vineyard planted on the field where wheat used to grow is seen. The judge who takes the bribe is seen. All of this is seen by the community—and by God. And there are consequences:

> *Therefore because you trample on the poor and take from them levies of grain, you have built houses of hewn stone, but you shall not live*

in them; you have planted pleasant vineyards, but you shall not drink their wine.

—Amos 5:11

Amos stands at the gates and declares that God sees clearly the unjust acts and even more clearly the unrighteous heart. Will Israel listen? Will we?

Will and Work

In Philippians 2, we have a great ancient hymn. This hymn begins with Christ giving up his equality with God to take on the form of a servant, a slave. No doubt, there had to have been many times when Joseph and Jesus experienced Roman soldiers and Israeli royalty who looked right through them. A carpenter may be important to a small subsistence village, but not to the people who subcontracted out their relationships with working people.

Let the same mind be in you that was in Christ Jesus,
who, though he was in the form of God,
did not regard equality with God
as something to be exploited,
but emptied himself,
taking the form of a slave,
being born in human likeness.

And being found in human form,
he humbled himself
and became obedient to the point of death—
even death on a cross.

Therefore God also highly exalted him
and gave him the name
that is above every name,
so that at the name of Jesus
every knee should bend,
in heaven and on earth and under the earth,

and every tongue should confess
that Jesus Christ is Lord,
to the glory of God the Father.

Therefore, my beloved, just as you have always obeyed me, not only
in my presence, but much more now in my absence, work out your
own salvation with fear and trembling . . . .

—Philippians 2:5–12

The most hopeful part of the Philippians 2 passage for me is verse 13: "for it is God who is at work in you, enabling you both to will and to work for [God's] good pleasure." The promise is given that God is at work in us to not only work for God's good pleasure, but also to will it.

As a Calvinist, I can do the work thing all day long. *Give me a list, Lord, and let me get at it.* However, this promise in Philippians is more precious than that. God is at work enabling me to will what God wills. This is the hope of every Lenten journey. At the end of the journey, we want our will to want more of what God wants and less of what we want.

What Does the Lord Require?

The Philippians text also includes another clue to our faithful response to God. As it says, Jesus "humbled himself." The word *humble* comes from the word *humus,* "ground" or "earth." Jesus came all the way down. Perhaps one key to seeing the invisible among us is to find the groundedness Jesus did. "Walk a mile in their shoes," our grandparents counseled. Another old saw: "Get down from your high horse." The perspective "from below" offers those who would serve Jesus a keen vantage point from which we might respond to cries for justice in our world.

Albert Bayly was honored as the pioneer of the remarkable revival in hymn writing in Britain in the 1960s and 1970s. One of his best-known hymns, based on Micah 6:6–8, is "What Does the Lord Require."

May singing this hymn help with our Lenten walk. I pray that our hearts might learn to will a life in right relationships and to see the invisible people around us.

What Does the Lord Require?

What does the Lord require
    for praise and offering?
What sacrifice desire,
    or tribute bid you bring?
Do justly; love mercy;
    walk humbly with your God.

Rulers of earth, give ear!
    Should you not justice know?
Will God your pleading hear,
    while crime and cruelty grow?
Do justly; love mercy;
    walk humbly with your God.

How shall our life fulfill
    God's law so hard and high?
Let Christ endue our will
    with grace to fortify.
Then justly, in mercy,
    we'll humbly walk with God.[5]

Chapter 4

The Beautiful Gate

One day Peter and John were going up to the temple at the hour of prayer, at three o'clock in the afternoon. And a man lame from birth was being carried in. People would lay him daily at the gate of the temple called the Beautiful Gate so that he could ask for alms from those entering the temple.

When he saw Peter and John about to go into the temple, he asked them for alms. Peter looked intently at him, as did John, and said, "Look at us."

And he fixed his attention on them, expecting to receive something from them.

But Peter said, "I have no silver or gold, but what I have I give you; in the name of Jesus Christ of Nazareth, stand up and walk."

And he took him by the right hand and raised him up; and immediately his feet and ankles were made strong. Jumping up, he stood and began to walk, and he entered the temple with them, walking and leaping and praising God. All the people saw him walking and praising God, and they recognized him as the one who used to sit and ask for alms at the Beautiful Gate of the temple; and they were filled with wonder and amazement at what had happened to him.

—Acts 3:1–10

With Glad and Generous Hearts

Every day we walk right up to it—that beautiful gate marking the entrance between the land of doing what we can and doing what we thought we couldn't.

The Bible says when you open that gate and give away the love you have received in Jesus Christ, something happens.

The earliest church, which began in Jerusalem at Pentecost, had a robust beginning. According to Acts, members were full of vim and vigor (Acts 2:42–47).

Peter and John were in the midst of it all. On their way to the temple to pray one day, they encountered a man lame from birth. Perhaps no one had noticed that he was lame early on. Like many parents, his father probably showed off his son proudly; his mother cooed him to sleep as he nursed. His grandparents probably made a big to-do over him, while his siblings treated him like a new toy.

The time came for him to crawl, he did not; to walk, he could not. The family realized something was wrong. They tried every cure, solicited advice, sought out the rabbi, and went to the temple—none of it worked.

His life took on a certain projection of few options. Asking for alms was one of them—a respectable way throughout most of history to seek charity for what life had thrown a person. According to the Old Testament, people were expected to give alms as part of their daily religious life:

Jesus healed a paralytic near the Sheep Gate (John 5:2–9).

If there is among you anyone in need, a member of your community in any of your towns within the land that the Lord your God is giving you, do not be hard-hearted or tight-fisted toward your needy neighbor. You should rather open your hand, willingly lending enough to meet the need, whatever it may be. Be careful that you do not entertain a mean thought, thinking, "The seventh year, the year of remission, is near," and therefore view your needy neighbor with hostility and give nothing; your neighbor might cry to the Lord against you, and you would incur guilt. Give liberally and be ungrudging when you do so, for on this account the Lord your God will bless you in all your work and in all that you undertake. Since there will never cease to be some in need on the earth, I therefore command you, "Open your hand to the poor and needy neighbor in your land."

—Deuteronomy 15:7–11

As the man grew older, his friends carried him to the temple at the Beautiful Gate to ask for alms, which is where Peter and John encountered him. The man did what he always did—he asked for alms. Peter said, "Look at us." The man looked at them, expecting alms. Instead, Peter said, "I have no silver or gold, but what I have I give you; in the name of Jesus Christ of Nazareth, stand up and walk" (Acts 3:6).

> **Merchants conducted business at or near the gates. Some of the gates of Jerusalem took on the names of the commerce conducted there.**

And the man—the one born lame who used to ask for alms at the Beautiful Gate—entered the temple walking, leaping, and praising God.

Let's freeze the action there and flash back to an earlier story in Matthew.

We Have Nothing

Now when Jesus heard this, he withdrew from there in a boat to a deserted place by himself. But when the crowds heard it, they followed him on foot from the towns. When he went ashore, he saw a great crowd; and he had compassion for them and cured their sick. When it was evening, the disciples came to him and said, "This is a deserted place, and the hour is now late; send the crowds away so that they may go into the villages and buy food for themselves." Jesus said to them, "They need not go away; you give them something to eat." They replied, "We have nothing here but five loaves and two fish." And he said, "Bring them here to me." Then he ordered the crowds to sit down on the grass. Taking the five loaves and the two fish, he looked up to heaven, and blessed and broke the loaves, and gave them to the disciples, and the disciples gave them to the crowds. And all ate and were filled; and they took up what was left over of the broken pieces, twelve baskets full. And those who ate were about five thousand men, besides women and children.

—Matthew 14:13–21

Herod had imprisoned John the Baptist—not because of his baptizing or raising people from the dead, but because Herod was keeping company with his brother's wife, Herodias, something that John the Baptist had a regular habit of mentioning in sermons. (It is a general rule that kings do not like to be told that they should not be doing what they want to do.)

One evening, while John the Baptist was in prison, Herodias's daughter danced so impressively for Herod that he promised her whatever she wanted. Herodias whispered in her daughter's ear to ask for John the Baptist's head.

Comfort Food

Jesus heard the sad news that his cousin and mentor was dead. He withdrew to a deserted place to mourn, as would most of us, but the crowds found him. Jesus had compassion on them even as he was seeking solace for himself, and proceeded to cure their sick. By evening, the crowd had grown to five thousand men and their families.

Most congregations provide food for those who are mourning—casseroles, fried chicken, rolls, cold cuts, pies—whatever is considered "comfort food." As a pastor, I learned to never eat before a funeral because the minister was expected to follow the family home afterward for the comfort food feast and storytelling about the deceased.

The crowd that gathered around Jesus did not bring comfort food—or any food, for that matter. They were far from home and far from being prepared to eat supper.

The disciples did what they tended to do best; they saw the obstacle in front of them—a huge crowd and no food. Their suggestion: send the people to town to get their own supper. Their suggestion would not have provided any food. However, it would have gotten rid of the crowd.

Jesus looked at the disciples and said, "They need not go away; you give them something to eat" (Matthew 14:16).

If I were to do a quick survey for food in your sanctuary, I might find some mints, crackers for the young children, and something scary in the bottom of a backpack. I would echo the disciples' response, "We have nothing here but . . . ." Of course, the rest of the story is the miracle of the five loaves, two fish, and twelve baskets of leftovers.

What does this story have to do with the lame man at the Beautiful Gate?

Doing the Impossible

Confronted by a hungry multitude, Peter and the disciples said, "We have nothing here *but* . . . " and Jesus fed the multitude.

Encountering a lame man asking for alms, Peter said, "I have no silver or gold, *but* what I have I give you . . . " and the man danced into the temple.

The gate opening needed to be wide and easily approachable for civil needs.

What happened—not to the man who was healed, but to Peter and John? Obviously, they had moved from being scared disciples to being emboldened in the name of Jesus Christ.

Every day we walk right up to it—that beautiful gate marking the entrance between the land of doing what we can and doing what we thought we couldn't.

Various theories abound as to which gate the Beautiful Gate was. The Nicaea Gate was beautiful, but no lame person could have gotten that far easily. The Shushan Gate was beautiful, but begging for alms there would have yielded little, since it was used for ceremonial occasions.

More likely, it was the double gate—the widest, with the most traffic and beautiful carved domes.

Sometimes, though, a gate's physical location is not important. It is the gate between what we can see, smell, hear, touch, and taste, as well as our silver and gold, gifts and smarts, and that place where we offer our deeper spiritual selves.

Entering the Beautiful Gate

On May 22, 2011, an E-5 tornado tore through Joplin, Missouri, destroying over a third of the town and killing 155. The deadliest tornado since 1950, it destroyed 6,954 homes and damaged another 875. An entire seven-story hospital was moved four inches on its foundation. Five thousand jobs were lost.

I visited Joplin with Presbyterian Disaster Assistance and heard miraculous stories, such as the one about Claude and Elisabeth.

They had lived in Joplin for most of their lives. He had been a bookkeeper at a box factory; she had been an employee at the county agriculture extension office. They retired over twenty years ago. They lived in a simple little house they had paid for years ago.

Claude is in his early eighties and legally blind. Elisabeth is bedridden from a stroke and has no cognitive abilities. They have no family and rely on neighbors to help them with trips to the store and such. On the afternoon of the tornado, they were alone, as usual.

They heard the sirens, but Claude knew he could not get Elisabeth into the safety of the bathroom by himself. So he got into her bed, lay on top of her, and covered her face with his hands. Their house was destroyed around them, but they survived.

A few weeks later, a FEMA worker discovered them living in a dirty store building some forty miles away that had been abandoned for decades. When the FEMA worker first looked inside, he could only see Claude in the light of a single bulb. Then he heard a sound and saw Elisabeth in the corner—in an exceptionally clean spot. Claude had kept her and her bed spotless. Because of his blindness, he had checked her IV by hand. Every night he had slept on the floor by her bed in case she needed him.

The FEMA worker could have asked his routine questions, checked off the boxes on his form, and gone on his way. Instead, he stepped through the beautiful gate.

Like Peter, he looked intently at Claude and began the slow, deliberate conversation of learning about this couple and helping Claude decide that Elisabeth needed to be back in Joplin in clean, accessible, temporary housing where they could receive help from their friends.

Open Now Thy Gates of Beauty

Every day we walk right up to it—that beautiful gate marking the entrance between the land of doing what we can and doing what we thought we couldn't. And sometimes we cross the threshold.

Some would say it is courage.
Some would say it is conviction.
Some would say it is hard-headedness.
Some would say it is recklessness.

Whatever it is, when we open that gate and give away the love we have received in Jesus Christ, something happens.

Benjamin Schmolck was a German Lutheran pastor and composer. In 1714 he became pastor of the Church of the Holy Trinity in Schweidnitz, where he served until his death. Schmolck suffered a stroke and was paralyzed on his right side. He struggled to recover and continued to serve his church. He also wrote the hymn "Open Now Thy Gates of Beauty."

While the text is of Lutheran origin, the tune most associated with it was written by a German Calvinist, Joachim Neander (1650–1680). The English translation is by Catherine Winkworth (1827–1878). Winkworth was fascinated with German hymnody. Through her work, she made countless German hymns accessible for the English-speaking church.

In addition to translating hymns, Winkworth advocated for women's rights and education for girls in Britain. She walked up to the beautiful gate and crossed the threshold. She gave away the love of Jesus Christ, living the words of the hymn:

Let my soul, where it is planted,
    bring forth precious sheaves alone,
So that all I hear may be
    fruitful unto life in me.

During this holy season, let us join our voices with Schmolck and Winkworth, and join our hands in prayer and service in the name of the One who calls us.

Open to Me the Gates

Open Now Thy Gates of Beauty

Open now thy gates of beauty,
    Zion, let me enter there,
Where my soul in joyful duty
    waits for Him Who answers prayer.
Oh, how blessèd is this place,
    filled with solace, light and grace!

Lord, my God, I come before Thee,
    come Thou also unto me;
Where we find Thee and adore Thee,
    there a heav'n on earth must be.
To my heart, oh, enter Thou,
    let it be Thy temple now!

Here Thy praise is gladly chanted,
    here Thy seed is duly sown;
Let my soul, where it is planted,
    bring forth precious sheaves alone,
So that all I hear may be
    fruitful unto life in me.

Thou my faith increase and quicken,
    let me keep Thy gift divine,
Howsoe'er temptations thicken;
    may Thy Word still o'er me shine
As my guiding star through life,
    as my comfort in my strife.

Speak, O God, and I will hear Thee,
    let Thy will be done indeed;
May I undisturbed draw near Thee
    while Thou dost Thy people feed.
Here of life the fountain flows,
    here is balm for all our woes.[6]

Chapter 5

The Gate of Total Commitment

After he had said this, he went on ahead, going up to Jerusalem. When he had come near Bethphage and Bethany, at the place called the Mount of Olives, he sent two of the disciples, saying, "Go into the village ahead of you, and as you enter it you will find tied there a colt that has never been ridden. Untie it and bring it here. If anyone asks you, 'Why are you untying it?' just say this, 'The Lord needs it.'"

So those who were sent departed and found it as he had told them. As they were untying the colt, its owners asked them, "Why are you untying the colt?"

They said, "The Lord needs it."

Then they brought it to Jesus; and after throwing their cloaks on the colt, they set Jesus on it. As he rode along, people kept spreading their cloaks on the road. As he was now approaching the path down from the Mount of Olives, the whole multitude of the disciples began to praise God joyfully with a loud voice for all the deeds of power that they had seen, saying, "Blessed is the king who comes in the name of the Lord! Peace in heaven, and glory in the highest heaven!"

Some of the Pharisees in the crowd said to him, "Teacher, order your disciples to stop."

He answered, "I tell you, if these were silent, the stones would shout out."

As he came near and saw the city, he wept over it, saying, "If you, even you, had only recognized on this day the things that make for peace! But now they are hidden from your eyes. Indeed, the days will come upon you, when your enemies will set up ramparts around you and surround you, and hem you in on every side. They will crush you to the ground, you and your children within you, and they will not leave within you one stone upon another; because you did not recognize the time of your visitation from God."

Then he entered the temple and began to drive out those who were selling things there.

—Luke 19:28–45

Palm Sunday

Is there any gate in the New Testament more precious to us than the sweet, idealized gate at the end of Jesus' Palm Sunday ride?

Palm Sunday is the day when we all get to become children at play—marching, waving palms, and singing hosannas. Many congregations begin worship with a parade outside the church building. In some communities, neighboring churches take advantage of this opportunity to come together in a procession— singing, proclaiming their hosannas, and waving to one another before they turn and head into their different sanctuaries.

On Palm Sunday, we joyously set aside Lent with the flourish of a palm.

We tend to project our own vivid images onto the Palm Sunday narrative, many times without even being aware that we are doing so.

In unguarded moments, the gate into Jerusalem becomes the chancel waiting at the end of the aisle for a bride processing into her wedding ceremony, her feet cushioned by rose petals as an adoring congregation looks on admiringly.

In trusting hearts, the gate becomes the Canyon of Heroes in the lower part of Broadway in New York City as the ticker tape and confetti mark a huge victory parade.

In our minds, the gate becomes a banner through which the high school football team breaks as they run onto the field or the Olympic stadium as the lead runner enters for the last lap of the marathon.

We might be hard-pressed to find any gate in the New Testament that is so precious to us. But is that its reality?

Palm Sunday marks the end of Jesus' long trip to Jerusalem and, eventually, the cross. The story is one of those few accounts of Jesus' life that appears in all four Gospels. Thus, it is interesting to contrast what is shared between the four versions and what is unique to Luke. For example, Luke's telling of the story is less ornamented and more subdued than the other three Gospel accounts.

All four Gospels mention the colt or a young donkey. In each, something is spread on the ground. For Matthew, Mark, and John, it is palms or branches; in Mark and Luke, the crowd spreads their cloaks on the ground before Jesus.

All four refer to Psalm 118, but for Luke the "hosannas" are left out. It is a disappointment, because "hosanna" tends to be our favorite

Palm Sunday word. Instead, Luke gives us harsh Pharisees who are full of rebuke, insisting that Jesus make the crowds stop. Jesus offers the curt reply "I tell you, if these were silent, the stones would cry out" (Luke 19:40).

Only in Luke do we read how, as Jesus drew near the gate, he paused, took in the sight of a city full of so much meaning, and wept.

> **The gate is a symbol of power, defense, and safety; to "possess the gate" is to capture the city.**

Truth be told, none of the Gospels specifically mentions the gate. It is easy to see it in our mind's eye and artists include it in most representations, but not one of the Gospel writers mentions it.

Triumphal Entry?

Needless to say, whatever version of the Gospel one reads, this event in Jesus' ministry is like an ancient triumphal entry by a king or a conquering general. He is escorted by the crowd of greeters; chants or hymns of praise are exclaimed; and marks of authority are bestowed, such as the young colt and the cloaks that pad the ground in front of him. While not all of the Gospel accounts make explicit reference to Zechariah 9, it is implied in all of them:

Rejoice great, O daughter Zion!
Shout aloud, O daughter Jerusalem!
Lo, your king comes to you;
Triumphant and victorious is he,
Humble and riding on a donkey,
On a colt, the foal of a donkey.

—Zechariah 9:9

So what do we make of all this? John Calvin points out that this brief passage on a colt is presented "not because [Jesus] was tired from the journey . . . but to show . . . the nature of His kingdom."[7]

The nature of God's realm. The procession on a colt is the embodiment of a scriptural prophecy, and the entry into Jerusalem is the fulfillment of a promise. It is the nature of this gate not to be a place of praise, but a place of commitment to satisfy an enormous sacrifice.

The Die Is Cast

As that colt carried Jesus to the gate, it was as if he carried him to his personal Rubicon.

You may remember the story of the Rubicon—how the Rubicon River in what is now northern Italy represented a clear border of authority, a "demilitarized zone" between Rome and the provinces it ruled. Bringing an army—even a Roman army—into this area was considered an act of insurrection. Roughly fifty years before the birth of Jesus, Julius Caesar deliberately led his army across the Rubicon to force an inevitable struggle between him and the lawful leaders of Rome—a struggle he eventually won to become emperor.

Julius Caesar is said to have commented as he crossed the Rubicon, "The die is cast."[8] Unlike Julius Caesar, Jesus did not enter Jerusalem at the head of an army. Instead, he was in the company of palm-waving, Scripture-singing disciples. This was no gamble by Jesus; the only people casting dice in this story would be the soldiers at the foot of his cross. Crossing the threshold of the Jerusalem gate, Jesus deliberately stepped into the one place where his words would meet people whose imperial and religious authority would lead to his crucifixion.

For Jesus, the Jerusalem gate was a gate of total commitment.

The Point of No Return

Compare the following lines from two hymns, both sung regularly on Palm Sunday. First, from "Hosanna, Loud Hosanna," by Jennette Threlfall, comes the upbeat, exuberant victor's march:

> From Olivet they followed
> 'Mid an exultant crowd,
> The victor palm branch waving,
> And chanting clear and loud.[9]

And from Henry Hart Milman's "Ride On! Ride On in Majesty!" are words that look beyond the jubilant processional into Jerusalem:

> The winged squadrons of the sky
> Look down with sad and wondering eyes
> To see the approaching sacrifice.[10]

Is the Palm Sunday entry a victor's march or an approaching sacrifice? The procession is both, but the gate of Palm Sunday is the point of no return. Jesus alone seems to understand that he is riding the colt across a line in the sand—a gate of commitment—that only he can make and must make for our sakes and for the sake of the world.

The nature of God's realm invites us, too, to cross through the gate of commitment.

It seems increasingly difficult for people in our society to make commitments. Some social scientists say that we are increasingly not "joiners." We are eager to contribute our time, our finances, and our energies, but we hesitate to commit to long-term projects, pledges, or membership.

> **Is the Palm Sunday entry a victor's march or an approaching sacrifice?**

The division, some say, is between being "spiritual" rather than "religious." Either way, the question is whether we are willing to commit ourselves to religious *community* and not just private *spirituality*. The word *religion* itself is about connection: *re-ligio*, related to the word *ligament*. Religion is a "binding together," a re-connection.

Commitment to the Way of Christ

Is commitment necessary?

I tend to think it is. The moment we commit ourselves to God with a trusting heart, we cross the threshold where we acknowledge that God is at work in us. We seek with intention to be open to God working through us to carry out God's realm of grace.

Making a commitment involves intentionality. Earlier in Luke, we learn of Jesus' intentions when he "set his face to go to Jerusalem" (Luke 9:51)—and now he has arrived to the cheering crowd.

We intend to lose weight, to stay in closer contact with friends, to engage in volunteer work. Those of us who are married may remember the part of our wedding ceremony when we declared our intention to commit ourselves to the vows we were making even before we spoke them.

> **Commitment is hard work and requires staying power.**

But we also probably know about having "good intentions" (speaking of which, how are you doing with your Lenten disciplines?). Commitment is hard work and requires staying power. Committing ourselves to God means committing ourselves to something larger than our own whims, passions, or priorities.

Walking through the gate of commitment, we enter into new territories of opportunity, for we no longer guide our own steps.

Walking through that gate, we commit ourselves to support our congregations not just as we wish, but also as we are called to serve. Walking through that gate, we commit ourselves to follow paths of obedience to the gospel and not just to our choices. Stepping into commitment, we step into a life that trusts the Spirit of God to bring us moments of discipleship we cannot imagine when we alone guide our steps.

The very word *commit* is, at its root, about connecting, about bringing things together. In committing himself by passing through the Palm Sunday gate, Jesus was able to engage the very powers of sin and death to win our salvation through his resurrection.

In the commitment of our lives to God, we become a part of what God is doing in this world that is searching desperately for hope.

We are being called to walk through that gate, acknowledging that we:

> Belong to God;
> Trust in Jesus; and
> Seek life in the Spirit of the Creator.

Jesus spoke about a gate to illustrate the difficulty of entering the kingdom. The gate was an elaborate structure with a roof and upper story and was often flanked by two towers.

Take My Life

Psalm 24 proclaims the approach of the Ark of the Covenant toward Jerusalem and calls the people to prepare for the Lord's coming. The Ark represented the presence of God.

> Lift up your heads, O gates!
> and be lifted up, O ancient doors!
> that the King of glory may come in.

Who is this King of glory?
　The LORD of hosts,
　　he is the King of glory. (Psalm 24:9–10)

Open gates, open hands, and open hearts signal a readiness to receive God's mighty presence. They constitute the threshold God crosses to enter our lives. Subsequently, the moment we acknowledge God's crossing into our hearts, we are given the opportunity to commit ourselves to Jesus Christ. We cross a threshold into intentional work and worship that intends to bring honor to God. Perhaps no hymn speaks of this commitment better than the old favorite "Take My Life."

> **Open gates, open hands, and open hearts signal a readiness to receive God's mighty presence.**

One of the most interesting marks of a good hymn is the way it can be folded into new forms of congregational singing. "Take My Life," a profound hymn of commitment that first appeared in 1874, has been given new voice in contemporary worship music. The text is unchanged with the exception of a chorus repeated throughout the hymn: "Here am I, all of me. Take my life; it's all for Thee."

The words offer an unambiguous witness of humility in commitment—for the one who sings them is not only offering all of oneself completely to service, but is trusting that, by God's power, "I will be."

That is what makes this hymn a good companion to the hosannas of Palm Sunday. As we put down our palms and walk with Jesus through the gate of commitment, we sing, "Ever, only, all for Thee."

Take My Life
Take my life, and let it be
Consecrated, Lord, to Thee.
Take my moments and my days;
Let them flow in ceaseless praise,
Let them flow in ceaseless praise.

Take my hands, and let them move
At the impulse of Thy love.
Take my feet, and let them be
Swift and beautiful for Thee,
Swift and beautiful for Thee.

Take my voice, and let me sing,
Always, only, for my King.
Take my lips, and let them be
Filled with messages from Thee,
Filled with messages from Thee.

Take my silver and my gold,
Not a mite would I withhold;
Take my intellect, and use
Every power as Thou shalt choose,
Every power as Thou shalt choose.

Take my will, and make it Thine;
It shall be no longer mine.
Take my heart, it is Thine own;
It shall be Thy royal throne,
It shall be Thy royal throne.

Take my love; my Lord, I pour
At Thy feet its treasure store.
Take myself, and I will be
Ever, only, all for Thee,
Ever, only, all for Thee.[11]

The Great Shepherd Gate

"Very truly, I tell you, anyone who does not enter the sheepfold by the gate but climbs in by another way is a thief and a bandit. The one who enters by the gate is the shepherd of the sheep. The gatekeeper opens the gate for him, and the sheep hear his voice. He calls his own sheep by name and leads them out. When he has brought out all his own, he goes ahead of them, and the sheep follow him because they know his voice. They will not follow a stranger, but they will run from him because they do not know the voice of strangers."

Jesus used this figure of speech with them, but they did not understand what he was saying to them.

So again Jesus said to them, "Very truly, I tell you, I am the gate for the sheep. All who came before me are thieves and bandits; but the sheep did not listen to them. I am the gate. Whoever enters by me will be saved, and will come in and go out and find pasture. The thief comes only to steal and kill and destroy. I came that they may have life, and have it abundantly."

—John 10:1–10

He Leads Us Home

It is the end of the day. The shepherd guides the flock from the pastures to the sheepfold—leading them down the hillside and through the village, past homes that smell like supper cooking. Along the way, the shepherd keeps an eye out for those young sheep that tend to get distracted.

When the flock reaches its destination, the first sheep go through the gate, soon followed by the rest until all are safely embraced by the stone walls of the sheepfold. On top of the walls are branches of thorny trees that provide extra protection from thieves. The shepherd closes the gate and the night gatekeeper assumes the role of watchful deterrent.

The sheepfold is a peaceful, pastoral place—with dangers looming in the shadows. Thieves and bandits, treachery and violence hover in the evening just outside the walls. Has the shepherd done everything possible to protect the flock? Will the same number of sheep that begin the night be there in the morning? When the shepherd calls each sheep by name, will each one answer?

When the shepherd calls each sheep by name, will each one answer?

Trust the Promise

When I first began in ministry, I served a small, wonderfully patient congregation in the mountains of Tennessee. While the congregation may have called me to be their shepherd, they, in fact, shepherded me through all the learnings of first-call ministry.

I was also blessed in my first call to have another teacher—Stan Rushing, pastor of the First Baptist Church in town. Stan mentored me in many ways, one of which was how to be a pastor at a funeral. Instead of fumbling with how to get the Scripture text right, Stan showed me how to get out of the way and let the text itself speak to the grieving family. Stan's teaching proved most profound for me in relation to Jesus' words in John 10:1–10.

Like most pastors in that small Tennessee town, I attended a funeral that Stan did for a member of his congregation. As he spoke, he likened losing the memories of the loved one who had died to the work of bandits. Death was a band of thieves that had stolen the deceased and robbed the family of someone they loved.

I won't forget Stan looking at the grieving family and saying, "Don't you let them!" Those whom Jesus has promised to keep are not stolen. The person who has died, has died in Christ and still has abundant life! The Great Shepherd continues to keep his flock beyond death.

How are they—how are we—kept by the shepherd? Three images in this passage offer insights to that.

The Sheepfold

The first image is the fold itself, which could be seen as the church or a worshiping community.

The dialogue is ongoing between those who find God alone—while hiking a mountain, for example—and those who insist it is by being part of a church community that God is most present to them. People like to say they are spiritual but not religious. They have a deep faith, but they do not want to be part of a church. Some of them may have some involvement in a congregation, but they do not want to become members.

I side with being part of a church community. In my experience, nothing is better for one's growth as a Christian than to be in a community of people where a four-year-old might ask you, "Where is God?" and an eighty-year-old might ask, "Were you at the mission fair?" Such communal interaction infuses our faith and keeps us growing. In the church, with all of its imperfections, I acknowledge my faults, yet am still embraced by a Christ-centered community.

Extraordinary people do not make a church great. Rather, the extraordinary commitments of ordinary people make it so. A couple opens their home to children from abusive situations. A family makes room in its life to help a refugee family. A busy woman sits all day in an emergency room with someone who doesn't speak English.

These examples of living service to God teach us, challenge us, and lead us to be better sheep, as it were. Their witness is a part of the Spirit-led, magnetic force that draws us to the church and keeps us in the fold.

The Voice of the Shepherd

The second image is the Shepherd's voice, the voice known by the sheep.

In the Reformed tradition, we banter around the word *call*. We are called to a new vocation, a new ministry, or service on a committee. More fundamentally, *who* calls us? Whose voice speaks to our hearts and souls? Whose voice has been calling us deeper into discipleship throughout this season of Lent?

Christ's voice has called to me and kept me throughout my life. When I was a young boy, my family would make a summer trip to the cotton fields of West Tennessee to visit my grandmother. I would spend nights lying in the bed next to her and listening to the crickets and bobwhites singing in the fields. On Sunday mornings, we, along with my uncles, aunts, and cousins, would go to the little Methodist church where my grandmother played the organ. She would sit upright and proper at the small electric organ to the right of the chancel, and she would always play some of my favorite hymns, such as:

Come to the church in the wildwood,
Oh, come to the church in the dale.
No spot is so dear to my childhood
As the little brown church in the vale.

My mother, who was a soft soprano, and my father, a strong baritone, would join with a chorus of cousins to create great harmony. They filled that church with sounds so bright and full of love that the sanctuary glowed—as did my heart.

Later, a retired minister would be the voice of Jesus as he challenged those of us in the youth group to respond to the call to deeper faith—and we all did so with little hesitation.

Discerning the Voice

How do we know when the voice is that of Jesus and not of those who would lead the sheep astray?

This text in John warns against those voices that would speak a false word to the church. However, I usually find that it is not heresy but the sounds of competing distractions and anxieties that carry people away from Christ.

Some of the distracting sounds are easy to name—the whack of a golf club against the ball, the zing of the fishing reel as a big one is hooked, the wind in the trees as a picnic blanket is spread, or the rustle of a newspaper as a page is turned. However, other sounds also steal us away—the voice of worry in our ears, the sound of tears or anger, the question "What does it matter?" and the artificial expression of false joy, to name a few.

Louisville, Kentucky, my home, is the venue for one of the largest festivals of imitators of the Beatles. Bands do their best to mimic the Beatles or to interpret their music in a new way.

However, I recently saw Paul McCartney in concert, and that experience was entirely different. Listening, I recalled that first appearance on the Ed Sullivan show, the many albums that followed, and more. I joined a choir of 50,000 that sang lyrics without any prompting. The response welled up from some deep-layered place of meaning and years of living.

To be clear, Paul McCartney is not Jesus Christ. Yet the difference between hearing McCartney's authentic voice and that of imitators is an apt analogy. Jesus is the true Shepherd; his voice calls us to the living God. His voice empowers us with the Holy Spirit.

> **Jesus is the true Shepherd; his voice calls us to the living God. His voice empowers us with the Holy Spirit.**

The Gate

The final image of how we are kept is Jesus as the gate itself.

A shepherd would lead the flock into the sheepfold and then lie down at the entrance as a gate. No sheep could leave and no wolf could enter.

Jesus is the Shepherd, the Son of God—the one who died, laying down his life for the sheep, and rising again that all might have life abundant. Jesus is the gate—providing the means to pasture and to safety, staring down the wolves of anxiety and fear that circle the flock, and filling our hearts with hope.

As the flock, we see the Christ lying across the opening of the sheepfold. Beyond the shepherd-gate is more freedom. Beyond the sheepfold, there is opportunity to graze with sheep that appear more likable than the ones in our flock. Beyond the sheepfold are greener pastures about which we've heard. But beyond the shepherd-gate is a world of uncertainty—and danger: getting lost in our freedom, grazing with sheep that are actually more disagreeable than those in our own flock, and pastures that may seem greener for a day but do not nourish over time.

This Christ lying across the opening is the Shepherd who compels us to relate to our own community. After all, the Shepherd created this community—where we live, love, and struggle to be the people God calls us to be.

I have been in church buildings, large and small, that range from the white-framed New England building with clear windows to elaborate cathedrals with ornate stained-glass windows. I like to walk alone in the sanctuaries—imagining the particular life of the congregations. I easily spot the pews where children tend to sit because of the signs of their leftover distractions. I see where the carpet is worn thin from people coming and going. I close my eyes and imagine the conversations, the hymns being sung, the prayers, the laughter, and the tears.

Our particular communities of faith are within the larger sheepfold of the one body of Christ. Christ is shepherd and gate, the keeper of this church community. Against this gate, the thieves of distractions and doubt, even death itself, cannot—and will not—prevail.

Our particular communities of faith are within the larger sheepfold of the one body of Christ. Christ is shepherd and gate, the keeper of this church community. Against this gate, the thieves of distractions and doubt, even death itself, cannot—and will not—prevail.

The King of Love

Psalm 23 is undoubtedly the most beloved of the psalms. Along with the Lord's Prayer (Matthew 6; Luke 11) and John 3:16, it is among the best-known passages of the Bible. The psalm reminds us at the most jarring moments in our lives, those times when we may feel most hopeless, that our God loves us as a shepherd loves the sheep. God cares for us and all people and provides for our needs. Psalm 23 reassures us that, all evidence to the contrary, God loves us, warts and all.

Reading or reciting the psalm at funerals is a popular act of faith, as the words of the psalm offer comfort for those who mourn and strength to live into God's certain future.

> The LORD is my shepherd, I shall not want.
> He makes me lie down in green pastures;
> he leads me beside still waters;
> he restores my soul.

Henry Baker was a prolific hymn writer who died in 1877 in England. His friend John Ellerton reported that Baker's dying words were from one of Baker's hymns:

> Perverse and foolish oft I strayed,
> But yet in love He sought me,
> And on His shoulder gently laid,
> And home, rejoicing, brought me.

The hymn is "The King of Love My Shepherd Is." It is difficult to imagine a better image than this to end our Lenten journey.

The King of Love My Shepherd Is

The King of love my Shepherd is,
Whose goodness faileth never;
I nothing lack if I am His
And He is mine forever.

Where streams of living water flow
My ransomed soul He leadeth,
And where the verdant pastures grow,
With food celestial feedeth.

Perverse and foolish oft I strayed,
But yet in love He sought me,
And on His shoulder gently laid,
And home, rejoicing, brought me.

In death's dark vale I fear no ill
With Thee, dear Lord, beside me;
Thy rod and staff my comfort still,
Thy cross before to guide me.

Thou spread'st a table in my sight;
Thy unction grace bestoweth;
And O what transport of delight
From Thy pure chalice floweth!

And so through all the length of days
Thy goodness faileth never;
Good Shepherd, may I sing Thy praise
Within Thy house forever.[12]

Sessions for Group Study

SESSION 1

Meeting at the Gates

MAIN IDEA

At one level, city gates mark territory, provide protection, and serve as gathering spots. At another level, they actually break down barriers. For Elijah and for Jesus, they were the place where significant encounters happened.

PREPARING TO LEAD

- Read chapter 1.
- Read this session and select questions and activities that you will use. What other questions, issues, or themes occur to you from your reflection?
- Each session includes a hymn. If you do not have a piano or keyboard, consider asking someone to record the music so that the group can sing the hymn with that accompaniment. The prayers in worship are taken from the *Book of Common Worship*. You may want to have a copy and review the sources. Feel free to adapt the prayers as needed.
- This session discusses encounters with widows, who were some of the most powerless and vulnerable in biblical times. Find out more details about their situation through a Google search or church history resources in your church library.
- Gather several images of different kinds of gates to share during this session. If possible, find images of city gates in particular.
- City gates level the playing field for those who pass through them. Human experience does, as well. For example, loss and suffering cut through all levels of status and circumstance. Yet the church is God's gift to us, a place where being present together gives us a sense of the gates; we are not alone.

GATHERING

- If this is a newly formed group, provide name tags and pens as people arrive.
- Provide refreshments, as well as a sign-up sheet for volunteers to bring refreshments for future sessions.
- Since this is the first session, form a group covenant that contains details such as maintaining confidentiality, being open to listening to all points of view, and so forth. Encourage participants to bring their study books and Bibles (though you will want to have a few extra copies of the study book and Bible at each session).

OPENING WORSHIP

Prayer

See Howard Thurman's prayer (Book of Common Worship [Louisville: Westminster/John Knox Press, 1993], p. 23) for a fitting opening to each session, or offer a prayer of your own.

Lectio Divina (reflective or prayerful reading)
Read aloud Luke 7:11–17. Invite all to reflect for a few minutes in silence. (Allow at least two minutes of silence.)

After reflection time, invite all to listen for a word or phrase as the passage is read again and to reflect on that word or phrase in silence.

Read the passage one final time, asking all to offer a silent prayer after the reading.

Invite all who feel comfortable doing so to share the word or phrase that spoke most deeply to them.

Prayer

Grace us, O God, with your merciful presence; wash over us with your peace that we may worship you through Jesus Christ our Lord, who taught the disciples when praying to say, Our Father . . . .

CONVERSATION

- Share with the group the images of different kinds of gates you gathered for this session. Invite participants to share briefly a description of a gate or experience involving a gate in their life (for example, a gate to a residential community, a gate to a neighbor's yard, or a turnstile at a stadium). Reflect on common characteristics of these recollections.

- Review 1 Kings 17:8–16 and Luke 7:11–17. Ask the group to compare and contrast the two stories. Ask: What is most striking to you in these encounters? What surprises you? What level of faith did the widows demonstrate? What difference do you think it made that these encounters happened at the city gates?
- Chapter 1 offers a number of ways in which we are more alike than different from one another. Ask: Where in the church are our commonalities emphasized more than our differences? What effect would it have if the church emphasized similarities over differences? What effect would it have in your own life? In your community? The nation? The world?

CONCLUSION

Invite participants to share common joys and concerns among them and within their congregation. Close the session by praying for each joy and concern named, asking the group to respond after each with "Lord, hear our prayer."

Hymn
"Stand by Me"

Stand by Me

Charles Albert Tindley, 1905

1. When the storms of life are rag-ing, Stand by me (stand by me); When the
2. In the midst of trib - u - la - tion, Stand by me (stand by me); In the
3. In the midst of faults and fail-ures, Stand by me (stand by me); In the
4. In the midst of per - se - cu - tion, Stand by me (stand by me); In the
5. When I'm grow - ing old and fee-ble, Stand by me (stand by me); When I'm

storms of life are rag-ing, Stand by me (stand by me); When the
midst of trib - u - la - tion, Stand by me (stand by me); When the
midst of faults and fail-ures, Stand by me (stand by me); When I
midst of per - se - cu - tion, Stand by me (stand by me); When my
grow - ing old and fee-ble, Stand by me (stand by me); When my

world is toss - ing me Like a ship up - on the sea Thou Who
hosts of hell as - sail, And my strength be - gins to fail, Thou Who
do the best I can, And my friends mis-un - der-stand, Thou Who
foes in battle a - rray Un - der - take to stop my way, Thou Who
life be - comes a bur-den, And I'm near - ing chill-y Jordan, O Thou

rul - est wind and wa - ter, Stand by me (stand by me).
nev - er lost a bat - tle, Stand by me (stand by me).
know-est all a - bout me, Stand by me (stand by me).
sav - èd Paul and Si - las, Stand by me (stand by me).
"Li - ly of the Vall - ey," Stand by me (stand by me).

Open to Me the Gates

The Surprising Gate

MAIN IDEA

Sometimes the gate shuts and the way forward is seemingly blocked. To find a way through involves listening to God and making oneself vulnerable in unimaginable ways.

PREPARING TO LEAD

- Read chapter 2.
- Read this session and select questions and activities that you will use. What other questions, issues, or themes occur to you from your reflection?
- Each session includes a hymn. If you do not have a piano or keyboard, consider asking someone to record the music so that the group can sing the hymn with that accompaniment. The prayers in worship are taken from the *Book of Common Worship*. You may want to have a copy and review the sources. Feel free to adapt the prayers as needed.
- Familiarize yourself with "breath prayers," which participants will be asked to write during the session. An Internet search will produce a number of descriptions and directions for this kind of prayer.
- Dependence on God takes many forms—people, location, circumstance, to name a few. What we do to stop, look, and listen for God is critically important when it comes to deepening our faith and trusting in the One who made us.

GATHERING

- Provide name tags and pens as participants arrive. Be attentive to those who may be newcomers to the group.
- Enjoy refreshments and either remind those who signed up or ask a volunteer to bring refreshments to the next gathering.

Sessions for Group Study

- Encourage participants to bring their study books and Bibles (though you will want to have a few extra copies of the study book and Bible at each session).
- Remind the group of the covenant made at the first session, involving, for instance, confidentiality, welcoming all points of view, and so forth. Ask if anyone wants to add anything to the covenant.

OPENING WORSHIP

Prayer
See Howard Thurman's prayer (Book of Common Worship [Louisville: Westminster/John Knox Press, 1993], p. 23) for a fitting opening to each session, or offer a prayer of your own.

Lectio Divina (reflective or prayerful reading)
Read aloud Joshua 2:1–11, 15. Invite all to reflect for a few minutes in silence. (Allow at least two minutes of silence.)

After reflection time, invite all to listen for a word or phrase as the passage is read again and to reflect on that word or phrase in silence.

Read the passage one final time, asking all to offer a silent prayer after the reading.

Invite all who feel comfortable doing so to share the word or phrase that spoke most deeply to them.

Prayer
Eternal God, you never fail to give us each day all that we ever need, and even more. Give us such joy in living and such peace in serving Christ, that we may gratefully make use of all your blessings in service to others; in the name of Jesus Christ our Lord, who taught the disciples when praying to say, Our Father . . . .[13]

CONVERSATION

- Ask the participants to think about a time when they were in a setting or situation that was completely foreign to them—a different country, a setting where English isn't the dominant language, an unfamiliar city, among those from a different religious tradition, and so forth. As time permits, invite them to describe briefly what it was like.

- Read Joshua 2:7–8 aloud, pausing between the two verses. Ask: Have you ever had a gate shut in front of you—literally or figuratively? How did it feel? What did you do? Who helped?
- Share with the participants that engaging in Lenten disciplines lends itself not necessarily to having a gate shut—though that can happen at any time—but to stripping off the layers we have built between us and God so that we see more clearly our true selves, faults and all, and realize anew our dependence on God. Ask: How comfortable are you in those moments when you are aware that your entire self is open and vulnerable to God? What does it take for you to get to that level of awareness?
- Ask the participants to identify those whom they consider to be among the most vulnerable in today's society. How might the participants serve as Rahab to the ones they have identified? What "rope" might be at their disposal?

CONCLUSION

Describe a "breath prayer" to the group. Allow a period of silence for participants to create their own individual breath prayers. Invite them to use their individual prayer throughout their Lenten journey as a discipline for becoming more aware of God's presence. Afterward, invite the group to join you in praying aloud the following breath prayer: (breathing in) "God of our lives," (breathing out) "help us to trust in you."

Hymn
"If Thou but Trust in God to Guide Thee" (*The Presbyterian Hymnal*, no. 282)

Justice at the Gates

MAIN IDEA

To align our wills to God's will is difficult, often painful, work. It involves identifying and confronting injustice in our society—and in our selves.

PREPARING TO LEAD

- Read chapter 3.
- Read this session and select questions and activities that you will use. What other questions, issues, or themes occur to you from your reflection?
- Each session includes a hymn. If you do not have a piano or keyboard, consider asking someone to record the music so that the group can sing the hymn with that accompaniment. The prayers in worship are taken from the *Book of Common Worship*. You may want to have a copy and review the sources. Feel free to adapt the prayers as needed.
- Collect a handful of newspapers, which the participants will use to identify what they consider reports of injustice in their own community.
- Injustices occur from the corporate to the personal level. Naming unjust acts that others commit is something we do with ease— perhaps even with eagerness at times. Yet our willingness to name the acts of injustice that we as individuals commit tends to be more difficult.
- One of the gifts of gates is that they make visible what or who is invisible. Developing the eyesight needed to see those who are invisible requires identifying and removing the blinders that obstruct our vision.

GATHERING

- Provide name tags and pens as participants arrive. Be attentive to those who may be newcomers to the group.
- Enjoy refreshments and either remind those who signed up or ask a volunteer to bring refreshments to the next gathering.
- Encourage participants to bring their study books and Bibles (though you will want to have a few extra copies of the study book and Bible at each session).
- Remind the group of the covenant made at the first session, involving, for instance, confidentiality, welcoming all points of view, and so forth.

OPENING WORSHIP

Prayer

See Howard Thurman's prayer (Book of Common Worship [Louisville: Westminster/John Knox Press, 1993], p. 23) for a fitting opening to each session, or offer a prayer of your own.

Lectio Divina (reflective or prayerful reading)
- Read aloud Amos 5:6–9, 14–15. Invite all to reflect for a few minutes in silence. (Allow at least two minutes of silence.)
- After reflection time, invite all to listen for a word or phrase as the passage is read again and to reflect on that word or phrase in silence.
- Read the passage one final time, asking all to offer a silent prayer after the reading.
- Invite all who feel comfortable doing so to share the word or phrase that spoke most deeply to them.

Prayer

Almighty God, you built your church upon the foundation of the apostles and prophets, with Jesus Christ himself as the cornerstone. Join us together by their teaching, so that we may be a holy temple in whom your Spirit dwells; through Jesus Christ our Lord, who taught the disciples when praying to say, Our Father . . . .[14]

CONVERSATION

- Ask the participants to define justice. Next, invite them to define righteousness. If possible, write the definitions on newsprint or a whiteboard. Discuss the differences between the two words, using the description on page 22 as a reference.
- Distribute among the group the newspapers you collected. Ask the participants to look through the newspapers for headlines or stories that answer the following questions: Where do you see stories of justice in your community? Of injustice in your community? Which are more prevalent? How easy is it to spot injustice? Invite the participants to share their insights.
- Ask the participants to read aloud together Amos 5:6–13. Ask: What was it like for you to hear yourself voicing these verses? How much of what Amos has to say is still with us in the present time?
- Share with the group that, in relation to the majority of the rest of the world, we in the United States have resources in abundance. In addition, statistics show that, on average, Presbyterians are among the wealthiest. Ask: What does it mean to you to be considered among the privileged in this way? What might the prophet Amos say to us?
- Invite participants to take a few moments to reflect individually on the discussion they have had. As they reflect, ask them to identify one thing they will commit to do this coming week of their Lenten journey that might help them better identify those hard-to-acknowledge areas of injustice in which they participate so that they can work to lessen them.

CONCLUSION

As a charge to the group, read aloud Amos 5:14–15. Ask them to pass the peace of Christ with one another.

Hymn
"What Does the Lord Require" (*The Presbyterian Hymnal*, no. 405)

SESSION 4

The Beautiful Gate

MAIN IDEA

As followers of Jesus, we are given regular opportunities to boldly put our faith into action—to step across the threshold from what we can do into what we thought we could not do. When we do, the results may be dramatic.

PREPARING TO LEAD

- Read chapter 4.
- Read this session and select questions and activities that you will use. What other questions, issues, or themes occur to you from your reflection?
- Each session includes a hymn. If you do not have a piano or keyboard, consider asking someone to record the music so that the group can sing the hymn with that accompaniment. The prayers in worship are taken from the *Book of Common Worship*. You may want to have a copy and review the sources. Feel free to adapt the prayers as needed.
- Putting faith into action means taking risks. It means ordinary people stepping out to do extraordinary things. How we work to deepen our faith during the Lenten season can play a significant role in how often we may step across the threshold of what we can do into the area of doing things we did not think possible, with God's help.

GATHERING

- Provide name tags and pens as participants arrive. Be attentive to those who may be newcomers to the group.
- Enjoy refreshments and either remind those who signed up or ask a volunteer to bring refreshments to the next gathering.

- Encourage participants to bring their study books and Bibles (though you will want to have a few extra copies of the study book and Bible at each session).
- Remind the group of the covenant made at the first session, involving, for instance, confidentiality, welcoming all points of view, and so forth.

OPENING WORSHIP

Prayer

See Howard Thurman's prayer (Book of Common Worship *[Louisville: Westminster/John Knox Press, 1993], p. 23) for a fitting opening to each session, or offer a prayer of your own.*

Lectio Divina (reflective or prayerful reading)
- Read aloud Acts 3:1–10. Invite all to reflect for a few minutes in silence. (Allow at least two minutes of silence.)
- After reflection time, invite all to listen for a word or phrase as the passage is read again and to reflect on that word or phrase in silence.
- Read the passage one final time, asking all to offer a silent prayer after the reading.
- Invite all who feel comfortable doing so to share the word or phrase that spoke most deeply to them.

Prayer

Gracious God, only you know the extent of our lives, the paths we will take, the dangers we will face. Give us faith and courage, trusting that you lead and love us; through Jesus Christ our Lord, who taught the disciples when praying to say, Our Father . . . .

CONVERSATION

- Ask participants to think about a time in their life when they took a risk. After a few moments, invite those who feel comfortable doing so to share their experiences. Then ask them to think about a time when they took a risk or stepped out of their comfort zone because of their faith. Again, invite those who wish to do so to share their stories. Ask the group to identify any similarities or differences between the first and second rounds of sharing and, if any are noted, what might be the reasons.

- Divide the participants into two groups. Ask the first group to look at Matthew 14:13–21, and ask the second group to study Acts 3:1–10. Have both groups answer these questions:

  What is the role(s) of the disciples in this passage?
  What adjectives would you use to describe them?
  On a scale of 1–10 (with 10 being the highest), where would you place their level of risk?

- After a few minutes, invite the two groups to share the highlights of their discussions and note the differences between the two reports.
- Ask the group to identify the qualities they think are important for a risk-taker to have. Record their answers on newsprint. Share with the group that the journey through Lent involves examining one's faith and exploring ways to deepen and strengthen it, especially as we journey ever closer to the cross. Invite the participants to reflect silently on the depth and strength of their own faith. As they do so, ask them to identify one quality on the list that they think they already have and another one that they would like to develop for themselves. Tell them that this will not be shared with anyone else.

CONCLUSION

Ask the participants who in their community and beyond needs followers of Jesus to be risk-takers on their behalf. Invite the participants into a time of silent prayer for those they have identified, as well as for themselves, that they might commit themselves to an even deeper relationship with God and to an openness to take risks because of their faith.

Hymn
"Open Now Thy Gates of Beauty" (*The Presbyterian Hymnal*, no. 489)

The Gate of Total Commitment

MAIN IDEA

The gate through which Jesus entered into Jerusalem on Palm Sunday was not simply a place of praise, but one of total, intentional commitment that would eventually lead to his death on a cross.

PREPARING TO LEAD

- Read chapter 5.
- Read this session and select questions and activities that you will use. What other questions, issues, or themes occur to you from your reflection?
- Each session includes a hymn. If you do not have a piano or keyboard, consider asking someone to record the music so that the group can sing the hymn with that accompaniment. The prayers in worship are taken from the *Book of Common Worship*. You may want to have a copy and review the sources. Feel free to adapt the prayers as needed.
- Commitment to organizations, including faith communities, seems to be a fluid issue in the current context of our society. Consider having conversations with your pastoral leaders or others for insights, trends, or resources that might be of help as you prepare to lead this session.

GATHERING

- Provide name tags and pens as participants arrive. Be attentive to those who may be newcomers to the group.
- Enjoy refreshments and either remind those who signed up or ask a volunteer to bring refreshments to the next gathering.
- Encourage participants to bring their study books and Bibles (though you will want to have a few extra copies of the study book and Bible at each session).

- Remind the group of the covenant made at the first session, involving, for instance, confidentiality, welcoming all points of view, and so forth.

OPENING WORSHIP

Prayer

See Howard Thurman's prayer (Book of Common Worship *[Louisville: Westminster/John Knox Press, 1993], p. 23) for a fitting opening to each session, or offer a prayer of your own.*

Lectio Divina (reflective or prayerful reading)

- Read aloud Luke 19:28–40. Invite all to reflect for a few minutes in silence. (Allow at least two minutes of silence.)
- After reflection time, invite all to listen for a word or phrase as the passage is read again and to reflect on that word or phrase in silence.
- Read the passage one final time, asking all to offer a silent prayer after the reading.
- Invite all who feel comfortable doing so to share the word or phrase that spoke most deeply to them.

Prayer

To your name, Lord Jesus, help me to bow the knee and all its worshiping, bow the head and all its thinking, bow the will and all its choosing, bow the heart and all its loving; through Jesus Christ our Lord, who taught the disciples when praying to say, Our Father . . . .[15]

CONVERSATION

- Share with the participants that a growing number of congregations observe Ash Wednesday with a worship service that includes the imposition of ashes. In many instances, palm branches that were used on Palm Sunday the previous year are burned and used for the ashes. Ask: What kind of effect do you think this connection has on the observance of Palm Sunday?
- Read Luke 9:51, explaining to the group that this moment in Jesus' life occurs shortly after the transfiguration and is the first

indication in Luke that Jesus is heading toward Jerusalem. Ask: Have you ever made a decision that changed or determined the later course of your life? Did you know when you made the decision that it would determine your course? Was there a point of no return? What role did your faith play in your decision?

- Read Luke 19:35–42. Ask: What do you imagine Jesus was feeling as he approached Jerusalem on the colt and heard the multitude begin praising God with great joy "for all the deeds of power that they had seen"?

- Invite the group to consider the phrase "spiritual but not religious." Ask: What does this phrase mean to you? Have you heard people use it before? What might your response be to someone who makes this distinction?

- Ask the participants to make a list of the areas in life that require total commitment—marriage, parenthood, enlisting in the military, deciding on a career, entering a twelve-step program, and so forth. As they look at the list, ask: From where does the staying power come to keep these commitments, especially during difficult times? How might the faith community be of support?

CONCLUSION

Remind the participants that this study will conclude with the next session. As they think about their Lenten journey to this point, ask them to give thanks for the insights they have had. Ask them to reflect on any disciplines they may have begun as they entered the Lenten season and what steps they need to take to continue one or more of those disciplines after the season has passed. How might this community be of support to one another?

Hymn
"Take My Life" (*The Presbyterian Hymnal,* no. 391)

The Great Shepherd Gate

MAIN IDEA

Jesus is both Shepherd and Gate, tending, guiding, and protecting his flock in life and beyond death.

PREPARING TO LEAD

- Read chapter 6.
- Read this session and select questions and activities that you will use. What other questions, issues, or themes occur to you from your reflection?
- Each session includes a hymn. If you do not have a piano or keyboard, consider asking someone to record the music so that the group can sing the hymn with that accompaniment. The prayers in worship are taken from the *Book of Common Worship*. You may want to have a copy and review the sources. Feel free to adapt the prayers as needed.
- Make copies of A Brief Statement of Faith. It is included in the *Book of Confessions*, which can be downloaded free at pcusa .org/media/uploads/companyofpastors/pdfs/boc.pdf. A major theme running through this chapter is the important role of the church in our work and witness as part of the Shepherd's fold. Spend some time reading about the nature of the church in the *Book of Confessions*. As you might imagine, each confessional document—from the earliest to the most recent—says something about the church.

GATHERING

- Provide name tags and pens as participants arrive. Be attentive to those who may be newcomers to the group.
- Enjoy refreshments and thank the participants who brought food and drink over the course of this study.

- Remind the group of the covenant made at the first session, involving, for instance, confidentiality, welcoming all points of view, and so forth.

OPENING WORSHIP

Prayer
See Howard Thurman's prayer (Book of Common Worship [Louisville: Westminster/John Knox Press, 1993], p. 23) for a fitting opening to each session, or offer a prayer of your own.

Lectio Divina (reflective or prayerful reading)
- Read aloud John 10:1–10. Invite all to reflect for a few minutes in silence. (Allow at least two minutes of silence.)
- After reflection time, invite all to listen for a word or phrase as the passage is read again and to reflect on that word or phrase in silence.
- Read the passage one final time, asking all to offer a silent prayer after the reading.
- Invite all who feel comfortable doing so to share the word or phrase that spoke most deeply to them.

Prayer
Eternal God, you have called us to be members of one body. Join us with those who in all times and places have praised your name, that, with one heart and mind, we may show the unity of your church, and bring honor to our Lord and Savior, Jesus Christ, who taught the disciples when praying to say, Our Father . . . .[16]

CONVERSATION

- Invite the participants to think about times when they have been "shepherded," perhaps by a parent, babysitter, youth group advisor, teacher, and so forth. Ask them to share briefly what that was (is) like for them. Note any similarities between the experiences shared.
- Ask: What is the nature of the voice of the Shepherd that continually calls you into deeper discipleship? How have you heard that voice throughout this study? How does your faith community help you discern that voice? How does it hinder you?

Open to Me the Gates

- Read John 10:1–10. Divide the participants into two groups. Have one group be shepherds; the other group, thieves and bandits. Ask the first group to list reasons for defending and keeping their flock. Ask the other group to devise ways to "steal" the sheep. After a few minutes, invite them to share what they have prepared. Discuss any insights.
- If your setting is conducive to it, invite the group to walk to the sanctuary. Ask them to take a few moments of silence to recall what they have seen, heard, smelled, tasted, and touched in that place. Invite those who wish to do so to share briefly an image or experience that came to mind. Ask: How would the images you have just shared or heard be different if you had experienced them alone?
- Ask the participants to gather into twos or threes and create an "elevator speech" (a message that is short enough to say in an elevator, usually no more than twenty to thirty seconds in length) that conveys the purpose of the church and/or why one would want to join a faith community.

CONCLUSION

Pray for the church around the world, for your particular faith community, and for each participant. Distribute copies of A Brief Statement of Faith to the group. Invite them to read it aloud together as a strong affirmation to help support one another through the agony of the crucifixion and on to the first rays of Easter morning. Exchange the peace of Christ with one another.

Hymn
"The King of Love My Shepherd Is" (*The Presbyterian Hymnal*, no. 171)

Notes

1. This is an allusion to Acts 16:16–40.
2. See Song of Solomon 2:1.
3. "Stand by Me," 1905, nethymnal.com
4. "If Thou but Trust in God to Guide Thee," *The Presbyterian Hymnal* (Louisville: Westminster/John Knox Press, 1990), no. 282.
5. "What Does the Lord Require," by Albert F. Bayly (1901–84) © 1988 Oxford University Press. Stanzas 1, 2, and 5 reproduced by permission. All rights reserved.
6. "Open Now Thy Gates of Beauty," nethymnal.com
7. Thomas F. Torrance and David W. Torrance, eds., *A Harmony of the Gospels Matthew, Mark & Luke, vol. 2, Calvin's New Testament Commentaries,* trans. T. H. L. Parker (Grand Rapids: Eerdmans, 1972), pp. 290–291.
8. "*Alea iacta est,*" attributed to Julius Caesar by Suetonius in "The Life of the Deified Julius," published in A.D. 121, paragraph 33.
9. "Hosanna, Loud Hosanna," *The Presbyterian Hymnal,* no. 89.
10. "Ride On! Ride On in Majesty!," *The Presbyterian Hymnal,* nos. 90–91.
11. "Take My Life," *The Presbyterian Hymnal,* no. 391.
12. "The King of Love My Shepherd Is," *The Presbyterian Hymnal,* no. 171.
13. *Book of Common Worship,* p. 500, adapted. Used with permission.
14. *Book of Common Worship,* p. 18. Originally from *The Book of Common Prayer of the Episcopal Church.*
15. *Book of Common Worship,* p. 20.
16. *Book of Common Worship,* p. 17.